Table of Contents

COLLOIDAL SILVER MADE EASY

DISCLAIMER: **I AM NOT A DOCTOR OR MEDICAL PROFFESSIONAL!** *I am however a 45 year old man that rarely had to go to the doctor in that 45 years largely due to my proven beliefs of the effect of*

Colloidal Silver on my immune system.

Colloidal Silver is a natural antibiotic has been linked to curing disease, sickness and many types of ailments since the beginning of time. In the age of mass plague and Pox many people thought that God hated the poor because when these horrible diseases would come through an area and wipe people out, the rich were often left physically unscathed by the tragedy. The reality of it was, the rich cooked in silver pots and ate off of silver utensils therefore killing the disease before it could do harm to them.

Most of you that are reading this already know the healing powers of Colloidal Silver so I will just get to the point and tell you a simple way to make it.   Following is a list of supplies you will need:

- 3 Nine Volt Batteries with connectors or 8 alligator clips with wire.

o   *Even if you have regular nine volt battery connectors you will still need two alligator clips.*   Distilled Drinking Water (if you are in a survival situation and there is no distilled water available, use any water available. Melt snow if you have to.)

- 1 Silver Medallion (99.9% Pure Silver), cut in half to make two half moons.

o   A hack saw makes quick work of this. In reality, two small pieces of pure silver of any origin is fine but a coin or medallion works great. Drill a small hole a little bigger than a spaghetti noodle right below the point on one end of both halves of the medallion or coin.

- 1 quart ***glass*** jar

- 1 spaghetti noodle

- Pure Saltwater Solution. (explained below)

That's all you need to make Colloidal Silver!

Page 1

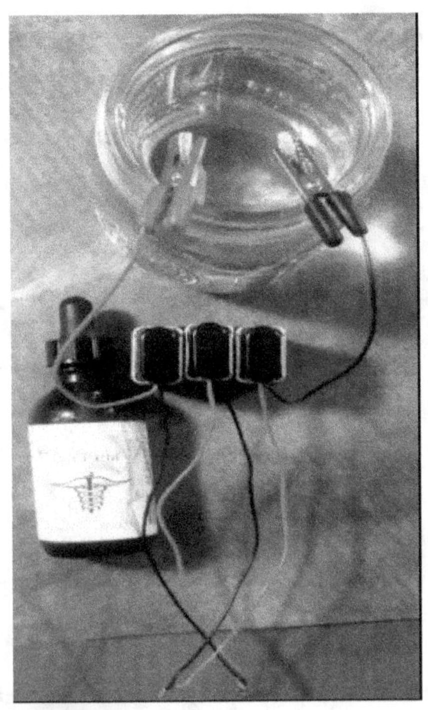

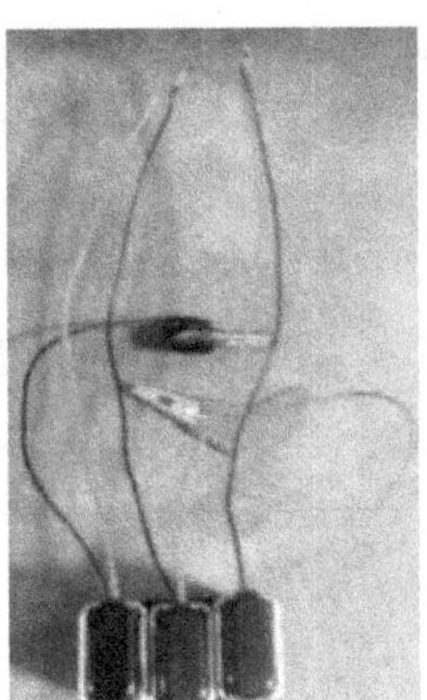

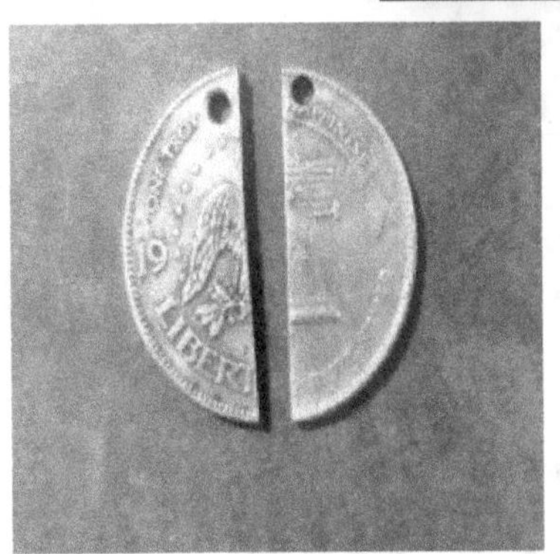

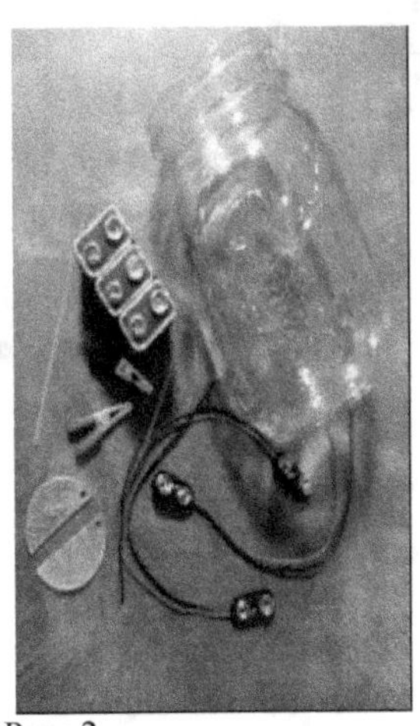

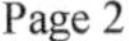

<u>**STEP 1: Saltwater Conductor Solution**</u>

Why? A saltwater solution aids in the conduction of the Silver into the water.

To make a saltwater solution simply . . .

1)   Heat a cup of water to boiling point and keep adding salt to it until the water will not absorb anymore salt.

2)   The salt will eventually just sink to the bottom of the pan and not be absorbed.

After making your salt solution, the best way to store it and use it is from an eye dropper but by no means necessary. *A cup of salt solution will last for hundreds of batches of silver and stores well so this step only has to be done once in a great while.*

After you have your salt solution prepared, it is time to construct your Silver Wiring Harness.

1)   Connect your three nine volt batteries together in series with either alligator clips or standard nine volt connectors with wires coming out the top. You can pick these up at any Radio Shack etc. (if you are unsure what "in series" means, please research it before connecting. In series basically means connect your first positive wire to an Alligator clip. The negative wire goes to the positive wire on the next battery. The negative wire on that second battery goes to the positive wire on the third battery. Then take the negative wire from the third battery and put your second alligator clip on it.) At the beginning and end of the series of batteries you need to leave about 10 inches of wire on the positive and negative side to connect your alligator clips to. In a pinch just connect them together in series anyway you can. Tape the wires on if you have to but regular clips are recommended.

a.   (If this part is too much of a pain or you do not have access to these connectors, you can buy the wiring harness and alligator clips all soldered together and ready to use from my Amazon outlet at this address: http://www.amazon.com/s/ref=nb_sb_noss?url=search-alias%3Dhpc&field-keywords=colloidal%20silver%20harness (batteries not included). Or just go to Amazon and type in "Colloidal Silver Generator Wiring Harness" and it will pop up.

2)   Grab a two quart or larger sauce pan and place on the stove over medium heat.

3)   Fill your quart jar to the rim with the distilled drinking water and dump it in the sauce pan.

4) Heat up the water just to skin temperature.

a. **DO NOT OVERHEAT!**

b. GET THAT OUT OF THE MICROWAVE! ☐ Microwaves will kill anti-biotic effects of the silver in the solution. **_NEVER_** heat it up in the microwave!

5) Put 10 drops of your saltwater/conduction solution in your quart jar.

6) After the water is up to skin temperature, dump it back into the quart jar with your salt solution.

7) Thread the half-moon silver ingots onto a piece of spaghetti noodle.

a. You can use anything that does not conduct electricity but I have always used a spaghetti noodle.

8) Drape the spaghetti noodle with the silver ingots on it across the center of the jar with the silver hanging into the water at opposite sides of the jar and about an eight inch away from the side in the water.

9) Connect one alligator clip to each half of the silver medallion. Set a timer to ten minutes. You should immediately observe a while milky substance coming off the silver and going into the water solution – **THIS IS YOUR COLLIDIAL SILVER!**

a. If you do not observe this chemistry effect taking place, make sure all of your connections are good. Some people wire a small nine volt light into the series so when the circuit is complete the light comes on.

10) After ten minutes, remove the silver medallion from your solution. You have just made COLLOIDAL SILVER for a FRACTION of the cost of purchasing it at your local pharmacy and KNOWING EXACTLY what has been used and added!

<u>CLOSING THOUGHTS . . .</u>

☐ **_Always_** *store your Colloidal Silver out of direct sunlight.*

o It is an anti-biotic and direct sunlight will lessen or destroy its potency.

☐ As for dosage, I personally will take a couple tablespoons three times a day when I feel the crud coming on. *I am not a doctor so I cannot recommend what amount you take.* Research it on the net for opinions vary.

☐	**Do not overdo it!** In rare cases people have turned a shade of blue from taking too much, but I have personally taken a substantial amount in my life and I'm still white as a ghost. That's all there is to it.

Good luck and happy health. I am attaching my email address below so if you have any questions feel free to email me and I will get back to you as soon as possible.

Crash.davis99@yahoo.com

Penicillin Made Easy

I must tell you before we get started that I am simply telling you one way to make "SURVIVAL" Penicillin. DO NOT USE THIS EXCEPT IN CRITICAL SURVIVAL, LIFE THREATENING SITUATIONS WHEN NO OTHER OPTION IS AVAILABLE! I cannot suggest whether you use it or not. I can only tell you what I would do in a SURVIVAL SITUATION and it is up to you whether or not you use it. Penicillin is so easy to make its ridiculous however if a licensed physician and a pharmacy is feasible, that is always the way to go. This is more of an invaluable survival tool in the event modern medicine is not available due to the variable strengths this concoction could result in. However, in a survival situation this information could save your life and is utterly priceless. Here we go.

1)   Take a piece of wheat bread. (Preferably fresh baked or bought at a natural foods store. But mostly important is just preservative free. Self respecting mold doesn't grow well on preserved bread.:)

2)   Put the wheat bread in a plastic container and cover it with plastic and throw it in a dark, warm place for a few days until relatively covered in blue/green mold(BE VERY CAUTIOUS OF OTHER COLORED MOLD. The blue/green mold is the color you want. If other colors are present, discard and start over) . (For a stronger Penicillin you can tear the bread apart after it is covered in mold and then put it back in the bag in pieces and let it mold for a couple days longer before use.)

3)   Heat a quart of distilled water up to roughly 95 degrees in a stainless steel pot. (95 degrees feels pretty warm to the touch)

4)   Add your slice of moldy bread. Do not stir vigorously. Just let the water soak in on its own.

5)   Cover and set mixture on heating pad that is on just warm enough to retain temperature. Let stand for 3 days. YOU JUST MADE LIQUID PENICILLIN!

6)   Filter your liquid into a dark colored glass jar or bottle. Direct sunlight can adversely react with your penicillin.

7)   Store penicillin in freezer for future use.

Again, I cannot recommend dosage but I personally would take an ounce a couple times per day for a week or so to fight off infection. This is however an antibiotic and any doctor will tell you that it is not a good idea to take antibiotics on a regular basis but as a last line of defense because your body will build up a tolerance to it and if taken too often it will not work. That's it folks. As I said in the description, this is a simple and short method of making Penicillin. Email any questions to me at Crash.davis99@yahoo.com Enjoy good health….

COLLOIDAL SILVER MADE EASY

DISCLAIMER: **I AM NOT A DOCTOR OR MEDICAL PROFFESSIONAL!** *I am however a 45 year old man that rarely had to go to the doctor in that 45 years largely due to my proven beliefs of the effect of these remedies*

APRICOT SEEDS

It never ceases to amaze me how modern medicine refuses to acknowledge the extreme benefits of many natural cures. It almost seems as if they would rather let someone die than try something that may or may not work. I would think that if you are a doctor and have a terminally ill cancer patient, you would try anything to save them. I mean really! If I was a doctor with a terminally ill cancer patient who was dying with modern cures being tried, I'd try jelly beans if somebody told me they would cure the problem!

I grew up in a home with a father who had a natural cure for EVERYTHING! When I was growing up I thought he was a couple sandwiches short of a picnic but as I got older, I realized that throughout my childhood, I never got sick. He never got sick. Nobody around him got sick for any length of time, and it was all due to his wacky cures. There is pretty much a cure for everything in a health food store if you know what to look for. I by no means know why some of this stuff works because I'm not a scientist but I do know it WORKS. And since my father is now 70 and acts and has the health of a 40 year old, and I'm not seeing any bad side effects, Im guessing this S@&T works!:)

I have actually done quite a bit of research on a few products however and a few supplements do stand out above the crowd. Of course Colloidal Silver,(see my how to make Colloidal Silver guide) Goldenseal and Echinacea are the ones that have kept me doctor free (except for stitches, broken bones and self-induced injuries) for almost 25 years, There is one "high power" natural weapon in the arsenal that stands out. Apricot Seeds!

Apricot seeds contain a compound called Amygdalin. Laetrile or B17 is simply the concentrated form of Amygdalin. I'm not going to confuse you with a bunch of scientific terms.

People read my guides because they are simple and to the point. If you want to know a whole bunch of scientific proof just Google Apricot Seeds and you will have all the information you can stand. Bottom line? *They are AMAZING!* I never took them growing up for Cancer or anything tragic like that. What I took them for was a last line of defense for stomach or intestinal ailments, food poisoning, or basically any bug that Colloidal Silver and the others wouldn't take care of.

I never make a habit of taking them first. Apricot seeds have a trace of Cyanide which always kinda freaked me out a bit but my Pa always said if all else fails take a couple Apricot Seeds. "They will kill everything but you!" I'm not so sure about that statement but when I started getting sick and nothing else worked, he was right! I would still recommend trying the first ones first though.

If you are just coldy and fluie they usually do the trick. As far as cancer goes, I have done a lot of research on this particular subject as it pertains to Apricot Seeds and everything points to the fact that they will indeed cure most types of cancer.

From what I have read a typical treatment amount that Is fairly standard for Cancer patient use is 3 or 4 kernels, 4 times daily. I however cannot recommend how many you take or even if you take them. I can only share you my experiences and what I do as needed. I use Apricot seeds as a prevention tool in moderation. A couple times a year I will eat 2 Apricot Kernels 3 times per day for a few days as a cancer prevention routine and other than that I only take them as last line of defense against stomach and intestinal bugs that I cannot shake with other remedies.

The instructions above for typical cancer treatments are more in my opinion for people that think or know they have cancer and are trying to get rid of it. If you do have cancer, please consult a physician before taking anything.

There are many fine alternative medicine doctors out there and thousands of websites to do personal research today. I would recommend doing your own continued research before starting an Apricot Seed regiment but they have kept me kicking for over 40 years and I know if taken properly will improve your health as well.

You can buy Apricot Kernels at most health food stores or online at Amazon or many online retailers. Be sure to read as much information as you can about Apricot Seeds before making a decision about if they are right for you.

HYDROGEN PEROXIDE

The other day I was reading over my Colloidal Silver making instructions that I have out there for sale and started wondering about how many people know the huge pile of uses for Hydrogen Peroxide.

It is such a simple idea that I figured everyone did but I started asking around and not many people actually know the many uses it has. Modern medicine has kind of damaged the general public's ability to take care of themselves. So I thought what the heck, I'll make a list of all the things I've used it for and a few I haven't but have heard of. Hydrogen Peroxide has many anti-biotic attributes as well as many purification and cleansing uses. I am just going to list them at random for your review but I will list the ones I have found helpful first:

1)   Germ killer- 3.5%- I dump it on scratches, cuts and wounds to kill germs before bandaging. It is SAFE! I use it on my kids as well.

2) Internal Anti-Biotic- Hydrogen Peroxide is a FANTASTIC anti-biotic! You need to buy the food grade however and dilute it. Food Grade Peroxide usually comes in around 35% and will KILL you if you do not dilute it down. I simply put a few drops in a cup of water to dilute it down and drink it.

3) Household Cleaner- Mix a standard size bottle of Peroxide in a quart of water and use it for cleaning everything from counter tops to that nasty funk in the bottom of the fridge. CAUTION! As with bleach, Peroxide will turn some things white so avoid fabrics etc..

4) Ear aches- I mix a solution of a tablespoon of 3.5% Peroxide and a cup of water and put a few drops in my ear if I have an earache. (Imnot sure how safe this is but I do it and it works so do at your own risk)

5) Sinus Infection- Same solution as number four but use for a sinus spray.

6) Teeth Whitening- Dip your toothbrush in standard Peroxide and brush your teeth.

7) Tooth Paste- Mix baking soda and peroxide into a paste. Works GREAT!

8) Tooth Ache- Mix up a solution of 1 tablespoon of Peroxide and a cup of water and rinse around the affected tooth.

9) Mouthwash- I mix a splash of Peroxide with water for a mouthwash.

10)   Kills mold

11)   Food Preservative- Mix a tablespoon of Peroxide in a cup of water. Put it in a spray bottle and spray leftover salads, meats etc. to save freshness of leftovers.

12)   Athletes foot- Douse affected areas.

Below is a list of uses I have heard of but never used it for personally. Research dilution mixture and side effects before using for these applications:

1)   Hair Lightener

2) Laundry Whitener

3) Stain Remover

4) Enema

5) Cleaning Contacts

6) Adding to air purifiers

7) Red Wine stain remover

I'm sure there are many more uses, but as a child and an adult, Peroxide combined with the amazing healing power of Colloidal Silver and natural supplements, I have managed to stay pretty much doctor free for many years.

PLEASE do more research on possible side effects of Hydrogen Peroxide before starting a regiment. I have used it for years for many uses described above without any negative side effects but I don't mind being a Guinea Pig. ☐

Below is my step by step guide to making Colloidal Silver (A $4.99 Value) that will save you a pile of money over buying it at the local health food store. Happy Health!

COLLOIDAL SILVER BALM SECRET RECIPE

Here is the reason I charged you another 5 bucks!

It took me forever to get this mixture correct so it would mix properly without separating. I tried all kinds of oils and balms trying to get them to mix without separating and here is the concoction I came up with that works by far the best.

1)   Melt one cup of COCONUT oil in a sauce pan.

2)   Add one cup of standard petroleum jelly and mix vigorously for five minutes.

3)   Add one ounce of your concentrated Colloidal Silver.

4)   Mix vigorously.

5)   Put into containers. Pretty much all big department store chains sell small lip balm containers and small cosmetic jars that work great for containers.

6)   For quicker use and lip balm and storage you can put the container into your refrigerator. The coconut oil will set up and make a firmer balm if refrigerated.

NOTE:*** If you want a denser mixture for lip balm, you can melt some bees wax into your original mixture.****

THAT'S IT! This stuff is AMAZING! It makes an awesome lip balm, skin antiseptic, cold sore cure, athletes foot medication etc…I try it for pretty much any external skin irritation and most often it works GREAT!

If you have any questions, feel free to email me and I will respond as soon as I can. Thanks…Crash…

Page 10

CRASH's CURE FOR THE COMMON COLD OR CRUD

I am NOT a doctor and I don't even play one on T.V!

However….I have not had a cold or flu kick my ass in over 25 years due to this simple regiment!

When I feel the crud coming on I take these simple steps and pretty much immediately feel better. If you follow these simple steps, you will be feeling great in no time.

SUPPLIES:

Go to the store and get the following:

1)   Emergen-C Packets or Airborne

2) Goldenseal Tincture or Capsules

3) Echinacea Tincture or Capsules

4) Colloidal Silver (Colloidal Silver can also be made at home. See my step by step guide on Amazon Kindle)

5) Apricot Seeds

6) BIG bottle of Merlot or Dark Red Wine. Everybody knows the healing power of Red Wine.

7) Ibuprofen

DIRECTIONS:

After getting above supplies, take the following plan of action:

1)   Open Wine.

2)   Pour LARGE glass of Red Wine.

3)   Take two large drinks of Red Wine.

4)   Open Emergen-C or Airborne and dump in remaining Red Wine.

5)   Open Goldenseal bottle and either squirt a dropper full of tincture in your mouth, or if you bought capsules, place two capsule in your mouth and chase down with two more large drinks of the Red Wine.

6)   Open Echinacea capsules or tincture. Put two capsules or one dropper full of tincture in mouth and chase down with two more big swallows of the Wed Rine.

7)   By now if you are following instructions ploperly, your Wine of Red glass should be kina empy.

8)   Refill your grass with Red Wine.

9)   Grab your Colloidal Sliver and put recommended dosage in the grass of Wed Rine you just poured.

10)   Chew two Apricot seeds if your crud is in your stomach and/or intestines as well. Apricot Seeds kill stomach bugs and this will help prevent crapping yourself if you drink too much Wed Rine and prass out.

11)   Apricot Seeds taste like ass so you will want to take the Colloidal Silver/Red Wine mixture and trink the rest of the grass rapidly.

12)   By now, you probably can't remember why you started this regiment cause you feel AMAZING and Im your hero so sit back relax and enjoy more of the bottle of wine.

13)   REPEAT every six hours as unnecessary.

14)   *OH YEAH! THE IBUPROFEN IS FOR WHEN YOU REPEAT STEPS 1 THROUGH 12 TOO MANY TIMES CUZ ITS FUN UNTIL COLD or CRUD IS GONE AND ALL YOU HAVE LEFT IS THAT LITTLE GUY ON YOUR SHOULDERS WITH THE BALPINE HAMMER GIVING YOU THE RED WINE HEADACHE you got withthis advice□…..Sanks and gud ruck…CRASH…*

SERIOUSLY though folks! THIS WORKS!

We all know that Red Wine is AMAZING for our body. This truly is the way I handle a cold or the crud (wine consumption varies but a couple glasses is definitely recommended) Between Red Wine, Colloidal Silver, Goldenseal, Echinacea, all the Vitamin C, Zinc and all the other great stuff I've suggested, a cold or crud doesn't have a chance!…□

Crash Davis gets his inspiration to write this stuff from his everyday life experiences and the people that surround him.Feel free to email Crash with any questions or comments @
crash.davis99@yahoo.com

These guides are for different areas however some of the tactics are repetitive due to this is a compilation of several publishings.

Outdoor Adventurer's Basic Survival Guide

Living as an outdoor adventurer for over 40 years and being an avid outdoorsman has taught me many things about surviving an emergency in the wilderness. Whether you are hiking in warmer climates or colder climates, there are a few things that never change as far as what you need to survive an emergency situation. In the following text I am going to give you a crash course on the necessities of survival in _MOST_ situations. This is simply a personal opinion based on my experiences and by no means am I the utmost authority on the subject but the things I list will certainly aid in your survival if faced with survival challenges in the outdoors.

First Things First .....

When heading out into the back country there are a few things that are of great importance when you prepare. Whether you are going snowmobiling in the winter or taking an ATV trip in the summer, or just heading out into the woods on foot, a few things are standard equipment.

Always remember, there is no such thing as a "quick" trip anywhere when headed out into the backwoods. Plenty of people die within a short distance of their departure and return location due to poor planning and preparation. Even on "short trips" you always need to plan on being stuck for a while for whatever reason. Anything from equipment breakdown to a fast moving weather front can leave you stranded for a period of time long enough for hypothermia or heat stroke to set in if you are not prepared.

Remember, a ten minute ride on a snowmobiling or ATV can mean several miles and hours of walking back through waste deep snow or knee deep swamp. The following is a guide of the *minimal gear* I would carry even on a "short trip" and listed in order of importance. The list is already assuming you are wearing proper clothing and have a first aid kit for the adventure and have told someone **RELIABLE** your destination and route . . .

1)   The single most important thing you can carry (and I NEVER go anywhere without) is **<u>FIRE</u>**! UNLESS YOU ARE IN A VERY DRY LOCATION, THEN WATER IS EQUALLY IMPORTANT).

In MOST survival situations FIRE by far is the number one life saving device you can have. I know some of you are thinking water, but <u>anybody</u> that travels the back country knows that water can usually be found within a few hundred yards of where you are. In certain areas of dry terrain, bringing water along is a must as well.

Waterproof matches are your best source of FIRE. Disposable lighters and regular matches can get too damp to light, even if they are kept in a sealed bag. Many are unaware that condensation forms in the bag due to elements and other factors.

Waterproof matches in a waterproof container are <u>always</u> your best bet. In a wet survival situation it is always best to carry some type of accelerant to get a fire going. Although it is a sin to waste it, that bottle of hooch you're hiding from your wife will make short work of starting a fire; the higher octane the better.

In regards to tender, in most parts of the outdoor world you can usually find a dry shrub or tree branch to base your fire with. Many types of tree bark pulls off in what looks like thin sheets and makes quick work of getting a roaring blaze going.

If the weather has been wet or exceptionally damp, I would strongly recommend packing along a candle. The flame from the candle is much more forgiving when attempting to ignite damp tender than a waterproof match that seems to burn at an accelerated rate when one is desperate.

2)   Second must have, is a good knife. A knife can save your butt in many reasons. With a good knife you can:

- ☐   cut limbs for a fire or shelter

- ☐   affix it to the end of a pole for hunting small game

- ☐   clean game, etc.

Although not as important as FIRE, a good knife is essential for surviving without having to re-invent the wheel. As stupid as it may seem to some people, a standard "survival" knife is not as "Rambo-ish" as you may think.

There are several options available on the market, and you can spend anywhere from $10 (at your local discount store) to $200 (at your name brand outdoor store). What you're looking for is a knife that has a hollow handle which is also a waterproof compartment. In this nifty hideaway you will want to ensure you have SEVERAL waterproof matches (nervous, cold hands OFTEN require more than 3 matches!), needle, thread, fishing line and a few hooks. Most of the knives I've described come standard with a handy compass as well, and the bonus? Sometimes that compass even works!

3)   Although water itself is *usually* abundant in the backwoods, you will still need something to put it in.

A metal can of some sorts usually works the best so you can boil the water after you get a FIRE going so you do not get Giardia (aka Beaver Fever) and wish you had forgotten the fire and knife and just brought a case of toilet paper! No matter HOW CLEAR the stream looks DON'T TRUST IT! Intestinal parasites can leave you dehydrated from "Oh, Sweet Jesus" explosive diarrhea and lead to your demise. Nothing else on this list will be of any benefit to you if you forget this golden nugget of wisdom!If possible, leave the food contents of the can in it until an emergency situation so you not only have a water container, you can enjoy your potentially last decent meal for a while. You might be surprised how good a can of green beans will taste after a couple days of eating fire pit shrew surprise. Your QUALITY knife comes in handy when opening your campfire cuisine, and I would strongly recommend practicing the fine art of opening a can with a knife in the comfort of your own home, where you are close to emergency services if necessary until you get the hang of it! 4)   A gun is next on my list of necessities.

Although not a mandatory survival tool, a small .22 caliber handgun takes up very little space and can make all the difference between eating roasted rabbit or grouse and eating something disgusting and too slow to outrun your starving butt like a Porcupine or Possum. Something a little larger is recommended in case you become the hunted. If you do go with a .22 caliber and encounter a bear, large cat or whatever is tougher than you, do not attempt to defend yourself

vith it unless no other options are available. Try firing in the air or into the ground at a safe distance or
ind a tree to climb to safety.(unless it's a big cat after you then the tree probably isn't such a great
plan!)J If you do plan on defending yourself against one of these large predators with it, make sure you
ile the sites off so it doesn't hurt so bad when the bear shoves it up your ass.

Always carry a revolver or single shot if you have an option. Automatics tend to fail when
stored for a long time due to corrosion from sitting. If your squeamish about carrying a firearm,
just keep it unloaded and stored somewhere on your machine or in your pack just for emergency
situations. Believe me, if you break down or get stranded a few hours from civilization, you will
wish you had a gun.

5)   Now a word about grub.

In a survival situation, if you have the above supplies with you and the weather is not extreme,
you should be able to survive for a few days awaiting rescue or better weather to escape your
situation. However, it doesn't take much room or effort to insure a few comforts if you find
yourself in a survival situation.

In most areas of the wilderness you are pretty much guaranteed you will have water. Dried soup
mix is a great way to ensure a little nourishment in case your hunting skills lack success. It
doesn't take up hardly any room on your machine or pack and even if you get some game it
makes great seasoning.

Although water is usually readily available in most areas of the outdoors, I recommend
throwing in a bottle or two of water just in case, and throw in some Emergen-C packets.
Emergen-C packs take up no room and they are great nourishment in a crunch. I get the part
about having enough room for beer and hooch but sacrifice some space for these necessities just
in case!

6)   ELECTRONICS!

I know you are all thinking that a GPS, a CELL PHONE, a RADIO and all the cool gadgets
should be at the top of the list but you are WRONG! If you have these things with you and they
work, that is AMAZING! Here is the problem with relying on electronic devices . . . *THEY
FAIL*!

Batteries die, signals get lost or are too weak, and transmitters go down. NEVER rely on electronics to save your butt! I'm not saying don't bring them if you have them, but NEVER rely on them.

7)   Shelter materials are of high importance as well but without the above items, especially FIRE, it is usually a band-aid on a crater.

A good tarp and a roll of cord is at the top of the list for shelter needs. You can typically find some trees or shrubs to tie the tarp to so you can get out of the rain or snow. A small pup tent is a better idea and can be rolled up in a very small ball and stowed easily somewhere on your machine or pack as well. There are a lot of good choices for emergency blankets that do not take up much room as well. In an emergency situation in the back country, the number one killer is the COLD! If you are in a high heat area, it still gets cold at night and you still need a place to lay down out of the dirt and bugs if you get stuck out there.

8)   If you are adventuring in a warmer climate that has lots of sneaky critters like venomous snakes and spiders, ALWAYS bring along a snake bite kit and "EPI" shot in your first aid kit in case you get bit.

So, Let's Review . . .

In summary, again, the number top keys to surviving being stuck somewhere in the sticks of the outdoors is keeping warm, watered and fed.

□   ___ALWAYS___ plan on being stuck out there when you leave and you will ALWAYS be ready.

☐   <u>*Always*</u> over dress (in layers) and try to take additional clothes with you in case you get wet or cold. Your feet are what are potentially going to carry you out of a bad situation. Warm, comfortable boots and warm socks are a great place to start. Your head loses and/or sucks up a tremendous amount of heat so make sure you have proper head gear. Wool clothing is always a good in the cold outdoors due to its warmth and fast drying if it gets wet. In the event you are stranded due to snowmobile or ATV breakdown, never rule out igniting the machine itself on fire to stay warm or signal aircraft or search parties.

☐   A good noise maker such as a whistle or air horn is a bonus.

This is just a basic description of how I, as an outdoor adventurer myself, prepare to head out into the woods (even for a day trip). By no means have I listed all things necessary for a 'comfortable stay' in the outdoors in a survival situation, it is simply enough to potentially save your life long enough to get out of the situation you are in.

Again, this is merely a reference guide as how I handle these situations and has kept me alive for many years in the wild outdoors. It is up to you whether you follow it. Good luck and be safe.

SAFE BOATING 101

<u>Preparation and SAFETY</u>

When preparing to go out in your own boat, there is one thing that you must remember comes first. SAFETY! It doesn't matter how many fish you catch if you do not make it back to shore alive. Always take precautions to insure your safe return. A boat is only one mistake away from being a sea, lake or river bottom ornament and you with it. Below is a list of precautions you should take in no particular order but ALL are important.

ALWAYS

ALWAYS make sure you have an extra plug if you are in a small boat with a plug. They tend to wear and fall out from time to time and this is a very dangerous problem.

ALWAYS have a bailing bucket.

ALWAYS have plenty of life jackets and if possible, have a survival suit for every person on board the vessel.

ALWAYS have drinking water stowed somewhere on the boat. Salt water is only tasty to the fish you are after.

ALWAYS have emergency food and matches stowed somewhere on the vessel in a waterproof container.

ALWAYS have a CURRENTLY inspected fire extinguisher!

ALAWAYS carry a first aid kit!

ALWAYS test navigation equipment BEFORE leaving the beach or harbor and try to have a back up signaling device or two. A waterproof hand held VHF radio and hand held GPS are always a great idea in conjunction with some flares and noise making devices. However, NEVER rely solely on electronics to save your butt! They FAIL! Make sure you have a plain old reliable compass and a horn and whistle on board to back up the electronics.

ALWAYS have some kind of EPIRB! (Emergency Position Indicating Radio Beacon) They make them portable and reasonably priced no days and there is no good reason not to have one.

ALWAYS have some type of bilge pump and a fresh battery on board. It is always a great idea to have a back-up pump as well.

ALWAYS carry a flare kit. Just because YOU brought a radio and safety equipment doesn't mean that guy 300 feet away from you has one and knows you are in trouble. AGAIN, NEVER rely on electronics to save your ass!!! SIGHT and SOUND!

ALWAYS have some kind of floating life saving device. I realize if you are in a 16 foot boat that a ten foot life raft probably isn't the answer. However, there is no shame in insuring your safe return by having at least an inflatable watercraft stowed in the bow. If you refuse to follow this rule as many do, at least take a pile of buoys with you and tie them to the rails of the boat. It does not take many decent sized buoys to keep your ass afloat for long enough for help to arrive. If you are on larger vessel, there is absolutely NO EXCUSE for you to not have a life raft. If you can afford the big boat, you can afford the life raft to save you and your friends or families life!

ALWAYS have a firearm. You do not need anything fancy. A single shot 410 is a great choice for a boat. Very safe, you can shoot big fish with it and if you get stranded on a remote beach you can shoot small game with it. A sea gull may even taste pretty damn good after a couple days of drifting around.

ALWAYS tell a RELIABLE person where you are headed and what time you expect to return. If electronics fail and your cell phone dies, this is a VERY important step.

ALWAYS carry a few tools and extra spark plugs and commonly replaced parts for your outboard motor.

ALWAYS carry extra clothes and rain gear. You are on the water. You're probably going to get wet.

ALWAYS check weather forecasts before you go. It can be beautiful one minute and blowing like hell the next!

ALWAYS take plenty of fuel. Take at least twice the amount of fuel you think it will take for your planned trip. Just because it is flat calm when you leave, it may get rough and take 5 times as long to get back to the beach or harbor. Running out of fuel in rough water is a dangerous situation.

ALWAYS make sure you have a good anchor and plenty of anchor line.

NEVER leave the beach without telling a RELIABLE person where you are headed!

NEVER go out if the weather forecast is nasty even if it looks good outside at the moment!

NEVER go out if you have ANY doubt in your mind as to whether the conditions are safe enough!

NEVER leave the beach or dock without EVERYTHING you need to return safely. If you forgot something, GO GET IT! The "I'll probably be ok without it" routine will get you killed!

NEVER overdo it with booze on the boat! Clouded judgment will get you killed! Save it for the beach!

NEVER take somebody else word about them "thinking" what you need is onboard! Put your hands on it before leaving!

SURVIVAL

Plan for the worst and you will have a better chance of surviving an accident in the water. If you follow the simple rule above you should be prepared for any incident that may occur. However, if you do get into a bad situation like I will outline below, pay close attention and you might make it out alive.

If you wind up dead in the water, the most important thing to remember is to RELAX! Getting freaked out doesn't help a damn thing and if you have other people relying on you to get them back to safety, freaking out just makes things considerably WORSE not better. Take a quick assessment of what you have on board and start at the top of the list figuring out what the first plan of action should be. If your boat is stable and not taking on water, ALWAYS attempt to contact someone else and let them know your location and situation even if you think it is a quick fix. If you are rapidly taking on water and the situation looks grim, and ARE equipped with any kind of EPIRB (Emergency Position Indicating Radio Beacon), activate it quickly, pop off a flare and then try to fix the situation. If you are taking on water, make sure your bilge pump is working and if necessary, and you have a back-up pump, get it working as well. After getting your initial "calls for help", and your initial damage control initiated, reassess the situation. If it was a leak causing your shut-down and you have stopped the water from coming in, and you think you can safely get back to the beach, head that way immediately! I don't care how good the fish are biting! If you have a leak, go fix it at the dock! If the leak is in a position that may worsen with travel, stay put for awhile and continue to try to get help on its way. This is a "your best call" situation and just make the best decision you can with the facts you have. Obviously if you have a crack forming in the bottom of your "pop can" aluminum boat and you have three foot seas, you are NOT going to want to try to travel far because the likelihood is that your boat could fall apart with the beating of the waves. If you are forced to travel, GO SLOW!!! Try to quarter the waves as to sustain as little pounding as possible and STAY in contact with someone else and report your position and condition regularly until you get to safety.

f you have a MECHANICAL breakdown, do all of the above except obviously you do not have a leak
o worry about. The first rule of Mechanical breakdowns at sea is, FIX IT AT THE DOCK BEFORE
YOUR SHIT BREAKS AT SEA!! Hanging over the back of your boat in 3 foot seas with an "IM
RETARDED AND SHOULD HAVE FIXED THIS AT THE DOCK" sign on your forehead is very
humiliating and dangerous. The sea is not a good place to maintain your boat. Always go completely
through your outboard before EVER leaving the dock! This includes checking the spark plugs, fuel
filter, wiring, fuel tanks, fuel lines, oil levels etc, EVERY TIME before leaving the beach! If you are
not mechanically inclined, have someone who IS do it! Take a few minutes when leaving the beach,
dock, harbor or ramp to just drive back and forth close to shore. Make sure EVERYTHING is in
working order while you are still within swimming distance.:) In the event you do get caught with your
pants down at sea, follow all the steps above in regards to safety. At this point, being embarrassed by
having to signal or call for help is still way better that being stuck out there. AGAIN, take care of all
mechanical issues AT THE BEACH! There are those unfortunate occasions where you did everything
you could at the beach and mechanical break downs still occur. In this case, just follow the above
protocol and then try to fix the problem. Obviously, if you think its just a bad spark plug or something
easy to remedy, you probably aren't going to need to set off your EPIRB but even in a situation that
you THINK is a minor issue, it is ALWAYS a good idea to try to let somebody know the situation and
your location.

IN THE WATER!

If you wind up in the water, with an upside down boat and nobody is around, and you didn't signal
anybody or tell anybody where you are going, this means you didn't listen to a damn word I just told
you and due to average temperature of water and the physics of HYPOTHERMIA, you are probably
going to DIE! My only hope is that you didn't drag any innocent people with you...Good Luck and
Safe Boating....Crash....

Halibut Fishing 101

Preparation and SAFETY

When preparing to go Halibut fishing in your own boat, there is one thing that you must remember comes first. SAFETY! It doesn't matter how many Halibut you catch if you do not make it back to shore alive. Always take precautions to insure your safe return. A boat is only one mistake away from being a sea floor ornament and you with it. Below is a list of precautions you should take in no particular order but ALL are important.

ALWAYS!

ALWAYS make sure you have an extra plug if you are in a small boat with a plug. They tend to wear and fall out from time to time and this is a very dangerous problem.

ALWAYS have a bailing bucket.

ALWAYS have plenty of life jackets and if possible, have a survival suit for every person on board the vessel.

ALWAYS have drinking water stowed somewhere on the boat. Salt water is only tasty to the fish you are after.

ALWAYS have emergency food stowed somewhere on the vessel in a waterproof container.

ALWAYS test navigation equipment BEFORE leaving the beach or harbor and try to have a back up signaling device or two. A waterproof hand held VHF radio and hand held GPS are always a great idea in conjunction with some flares and noise making devices. However, NEVER rely solely on electronics to save your butt! They FAIL! Make sure you have a plain old reliable compass and a horn and whistle on board to back up the electronics.

ALWAYS have some kind of floating life saving device. I realize if you are in a 16 foot boat that a ten foot life raft probably isn't the answer. However, there is no shame in insuring your safe return by having at least an inflatable watercraft stowed in the bow. If you refuse to follow this rule as many do, at least take a pile of buoys with you and tie them to the rails of the boat. It does not take many decent sized buoys to keep your ass afloat for long enough for help to arrive. If you are on larger vessel, there is absolutely NO EXCUSE for you to not have a life raft. If you can afford the big boat, you can afford the life raft to save you and your friends or families life!

ALWAYS have a firearm. You do not need anything fancy. A single shot 410 is a great choice for a boat. Very safe, you can shoot big Halibut with it and if you get stranded on a remote beach you can shoot small game with it. A sea gull may even taste pretty damn good after a couple days of drifting around.

ALWAYS tell a RELIABLE person where you are headed and what time you expect to return. If electronics fail and your cell phone dies, this is a VERY important step.

ALWAYS carry a few tools and extra spark plugs and commonly replaced parts for your outboard motor.

ALWAYS carry extra clothes and rain gear. You are on the water. You're probably going to get wet.

ALWAYS check weather forecasts before you go. It can be beautiful one minute and blowing like hell the next!

ALWAYS take plenty of fuel. Take at least twice the amount of fuel you think it will take for your planned trip. Just because it is flat calm when you leave, it may get rough and take 5 times as long to get back to the beach or harbor. Running out of fuel in rough water is a dangerous situation.

ALWAYS make sure you have a good anchor and plenty of anchor line.

Fishing Gear

1)   Halibut Rod- Depending on what your mission of the day is, choose your rod accordingly. If you are "meat" fishing, a good short and stiff rod that will hold up to 100lb or more test heavy duty line is what you need. If you are going for the sportsman aspect, I suggest a medium size trolling rod that will hold up to some 25 to 40 lb test monofilament line. I personally use a Lami-glas, Kenai King or equivalent. You can feel the fish bite better and it's a lot more fun. I have caught more large Halibut on a Salmon rod than a Halibut rod and had way more fun doing it.

2) Halibut Reel- As I talked about above, if you are "meat" fishing, a heavy duty level wind reel that will hold a couple hundred yards of 100+ Lb test is the way to go. Penn probably makes your best all around, reasonably priced Halibut reels. For smaller sporting Halibut reels, there is a wide variety to choose from but any reputable companies levelwind that will hold a few hundred yards of 25 to 40 Lb test monofilament line will be fine.

3) Harpoon- Always carry a harpoon. Even with smaller Halibut, it just makes them easier to manage with a harpoon stuck through them. I always say, "harpoon them and you own them". (except for the time I harpooned a couple hundred pounder and then right directly shot my line and the harpoon cable in half with a .357 while attempting to kill the Halibut. No tips that day!:) Therein the .410 scattergun is a much better weapon of choice for a boat.) However, when harpooning a large Halibut in a small boat, NEVER tie the harpoon line to the boat. A large Halibut will sink your ass! Tie the end to a buoy and in the event the fish is unmanageable, toss the whole works overboard. (after making sure the line is not wrapped around your ankle of course) The fish will eventually come back to the surface with the buoy and you can easily grab it then.

4) Bait- Although Halibut will eat pretty much anything you throw at them when they are in abundance under the boat, you will want to bring a few options for bait for slow times. Due to certain situations that I will explain later on in this guide you will want to bring the following at a minimum.

Large Herring

Small Troll Herring

Octopus or Squid

5) Tackle- Halibut tackle is pretty basic. If you have some large circle hooks and J hooks, some 1 to 3 Lb lead balls, large sliders and barrel swivels in your box, you are pretty much ready to go Halibut fishing. The only real exception to this rule is some smaller hooks and sinkers if you decide to go the sportsman route instead of the "meat" fisherman route.

6) Depth Sounder and Chart- You need to have a good chart that shows bottom depth and terrain. Even if you do not have a GPS, you can still judge distance by sight and by using your depth finder you can accurately find a good spot to fish.

There a few important keys to the success of Halibut fishing. Number one is LOCATION. Before leaving the port or beach, pull out your chart and find a good location to head for. If you are in a small boat, always look for the closest yet most productive looking area you can because if the weather gets rough you can get back to port faster. Although it is not a guy thing to do, if you are in a location you have not been before, ask somebody like a charter boat operator where the closest place to catch decent Halibut is. After deciding on a spot to head for, take a mental check list of things on board to insure your safe return and head out. Halibut tend to live in numbers anywhere you can find a decent shelf. Deeper water does not necessarily mean more Halibut so going 50 miles out definitely will not increase your luck if there is good areas closer. If you find a good shelf to fish reasonably close to port, head that way and give it a try. You can always move if it sucks. Finding these close spots usually is not rocket science because when you get anywhere close, there will be other boats scattered around the site. This is never a bad thing due to several reasons. The number one reason is SAFETY. The number two reason is that HALIBUT go where the food is and with a bunch of boats around, there is plenty of food already in the water. Its kind of a cheap shot but always go down tide of the other boats if you can find good terrain there because that is the way the other boats scent from their bait is traveling and you can cut the fish off at the pass.:) If there are no other boats in the area you want to fish, anchor or drift the area just on the edge of the shelf first. Halibut tend to hang out more on the edge than on the top itself. IF YOU DO ANCHOR, ALWAYS BE EXTREMELY CAREFUL! THIS IS THE MOST DANGEROUS PART OF THE TRIP. MORE PEOPLE HAVE SANK IN MORE SMALL BOATS FROM IMPROPER ANCHORING AND IMPROPPER PULLING OF THE ANCHOR THAN CARTER HAS LIVER PILLS.

Another important aspect of Halibut fishing is TIDE. Extreme high and low tides with high volumes of water moving are a pain in the ass to fish. Try to plan your trips when there is not a big difference in water volume movement from high to low tide. The biggest "wives tale" you will hear is that "SLACK" tide is the time to catch Halibut. This is WRONG! The time surrounding slack tide is however a great time to fish Halibut. You want some water moving to mask your bait,hook and line and to carry scent around your location to bring in the fish. Completely slack tide is a great time to eat lunch! There is a way to liven up the action however that I will talk about in a bit. After you find your spot and are anchored or ready to fish here are some tips on how to catch a Halibut….

When you are ready to fish, here are some tips to insure your success. If you are a patient fisherman that just throws your rod in a holder, go with a circle hook. If you are a "johnny on it" fisherman, or kids, go with a J hook (jerk hook). For the sportsman and the light tackle, a smaller (2 O) hood is recommended. If you are using light tackle, do not use expensive hooks because you will go through a bunch of them on trash fish. Mustad makes a good cheaper hook and sold by the box. In all cases, you will want to rig up your gear by putting a weight slider above a barrel swivel and then tie your hook about two feet below your sinker. Some people prefer to use a three way swivel and tie your weight on a leader that hangs off the bottom of the three way swivel and keeps your bait up off the bottom a little bit. I have tried it both ways and I prefer just a straight line. After getting your gear tied on and choosing a weight that is appropriate for the amount of tide moving, pick your bait. For "meat" fishing on the large poles, I always put a small piece of Octopus or Squid on the hook first, followed by a piece of Herring. Especially in deeper water because a Halibut is pretty crafty and will often get the Herring off your hook with ease but the Octopus or Squid will hang on for a second or third attempt. I prefer the Herring as part of the package due to lots of oil and scent. The Octopus and Squid are tough but not much scent. It is never a bad idea to have some extra scent oils handy if fishing is slow. For the smaller sportsman rods, use a double hook set up and put a troll herring on for bait. This set up is by far going to out fish the larger rigs for several reasons. Most importantly I believe is because the Halibut cannot sense the smaller line and hooks in the water. Secondly, you attract a lot more smaller fish that creates a feeding frenzy for the larger fish. Even if you are "meat" fishing, ALWAYS keep a smaller rod and reel on the boat for slow times. They are a HUGE asset to your success. Always begin your fishing with somebody on the boat using the light tackle. It always creates better fishing. And for kids, you can't beat it because there is always something chewing on the small gear. And at SLACK tide when NOTHING else works, the smaller gear will work because the Halibut have a harder time sensing the gear.

Keep the gear moving! Always keep your bait moving around the bottom with a constant motion with occasional lapses in movement so the big, slow fish can grab your bait. When the tide starts to move pretty good, this is not always a bad thing. Just let your bait bounce back and out a little at a time. Especially with larger gear, this can be more productive due to the fish not sensing the large line and hook.

Typically if you haven't had a bite within a half an hour or so, especially if you have the small rod out, you are in the wrong spot. Don't waste the day on a spot you think should be great but isn't. Move to a new spot. If you run out of ideas and are frustrated, go back to plan A! I guarantee if you can find a few charter boats dog piled up somewhere on the horizon, there are fish there. Go there! There is less shame in joining the dog pile than going home and telling your wife you just plain suck and she will be a lot more apt to let you go fishing more often if you are bringing home dinner even if you had to rob it out from under a charter boats keel□!

With these simple ideas and tips I have laid out for you, there is no reason you cannot have a safe and successful Halibut fishing adventure. Although I have been fishing Halibut in many different waters for over 40 years, I always recommend talking to someone local to the area you are planning on fishing to get local knowledge of any dangers or advice they can give you. Thanks for reading and good luck and most importantly BE SAFE out there!

SALTWATER SALMON FISHING

Fishing Gear

I suggest a medium size trolling rod that will handle 25 to 40 lb test monofilament line. I personally use a Lami-Glas, Kenai King or equivalent. You can feel the fish bite better and it's a lot more fun.

1)   King Salmon Reel-There are a wide variety of good reels to choose from but any reputable companies levelwind that will hold a few hundred yards of 25 to 40 Lb test monofilament line will be fine.

2) Harpoon- Always carry a harpoon in case you troll into a Halibut, it just makes them easier to manage with a harpoon stuck through them. I always say, "harpoon them and you own them". (except for the time I harpooned a couple hundred pounder and then right directly shot my line and the harpoon cable in half with a .357 while attempting to kill the Halibut. No tips that day!:) Therein the .410 scattergun is a much better weapon of choice for a boat.) However, when harpooning a large Halibut in a small boat, NEVER tie the harpoon line to the boat. A large Halibut will sink your ass! Tie the end to a buoy and in the event the fish is unmanageable, toss the whole works overboard. (after making sure the line is not wrapped around your ankle of course) The fish will eventually come back to the surface with the buoy and you can easily grab it then.

3) Bait- King Salmon will eat pretty much anything in the ocean that will fit in their mouth when they are in abundance under the boat, you will want to bring a few options for bait for slow times. Due to certain situations that I will explain later on in this guide you will want to bring the following at a minimum.

Troll Herring

Herring or Sardine Oil

4) Tackle- King Salmon tackle for the ocean is pretty basic. If you have some double single hook rigs, large spinners such as Tee- Spoons, Skagit Specials etc, in a variety of colors you will be ok. Medium size sinker sliders with a variety of small sinkers and barrel and snap swivels in your box are a must as well. Do not buy cheap swivels! You are begging for a problem if you do!

5) Net- Always make sure you grab the net before you head out. Many times in my younger days I hooked into Kings and went to grab my net and the back of my truck was too far away! It happens more often that you think!:)

Lets Go Fishing!!!

There a few important keys to the success of King Salmon fishing. Number one is LOCATION. Before leaving the port or beach, pull out your chart and find a good location to head for. If you are in a small boat, always look for the closest yet most productive looking area you can because if the weather gets rough you can get back to port faster. Although it is not a guy thing to do, if you are in a location you have not been before, ask somebody like a charter boat operator where the closest place to catch decent Kings is. Typically they are going to lie to you but it's worth a shot. If you are in a brand new area, just get up early, ask around about who is the best guide service, find their boats and follow them to the grounds. It AIN'T rocket science and at 5 bucks a gallon for fuel, it will save you a bundle of money that can be spent on more important things like beer! After deciding on a spot to head for, take a mental check list of things on board to insure your safe return and head out. King Salmon tend to congregate close to the beach on their way to their river of destination. There are exceptions to this rule however. "Feeder" Kings are the ones that will stay out deeper because they are not headed for a river to spawn in. They are simply living and feeding at different locations before their trip to a spawning stream. These Kings are best caught with downriggers and troll herring or by simply dropping a troll Herring to the bottom and mooching for them.Deeper water does not necessarily mean more Kings so going 50 miles out definitely will not increase your luck if there are good areas closer. If you find a good area to fish reasonably close to port, head that way and give it a try. You can always move if it sucks. Finding these close spots usually is not rocket science because when you get anywhere close, there will be other boats scattered around the site. This is never a bad thing due to several reasons. The number one reason is SAFETY. The number two reason is that Kings go where the food is and with a bunch of boats around, there is plenty of food already in the water. Its kind of a cheap shot but always go down tide of the other boats if you can find good terrain there because that is the way the other boats scent from their bait is traveling and you can cut the fish off at the pass.:) IF YOU DO ANCHOR AND MOOCH FOR KINGS AND HALIBUT, ALWAYS BE EXTREMELY CAREFUL! THIS IS THE MOST DANGEROUS PART OF THE TRIP. MORE PEOPLE HAVE SANK IN MORE SMALL BOATS FROM IMPROPER ANCHORING AND IMPROPPER PULLING OF THE ANCHOR THAN CARTER HAS LIVER PILLS. DO NOT TRY USING THE BOUY TO PULL YOUR ANCHOR WITHOUT A TRAINED PERSON SHOWING YOU HOW TO DO IT. YOU WILL WIND UP WITH THE ANCHOR LINE IN YOUR PROP AT THE VERY LEAST AND AT THE BOTTOM OF THE OCEAN AT THE WORST!!!!

Another important aspect of King fishing is TIDE. Extreme high and low tides with high volumes of water moving are a pain in the ass to fish. Try to plan your trips when there is not a big difference in water volume movement from high to low tide. The biggest "wives tale" you will hear is that "SLACK" tide is the time to catch Kings. This is WRONG! The time surrounding slack tide is however a great time to fish Kings. You want some water moving to mask your bait,hook and line and to carry scent around your location to bring in the fish. Completely slack tide is a great time to eat lunch! There is a way to liven up the action however that I will talk about in a bit.

FISHING for King Salmon

When you find your spot and are ready to fish, here are some tips to insure your success. Keep in mind that King fishing from a boat is often a very tedious and somewhat boring venture. You can spend hours in search of that first strike. Don't give up though! It only takes a second to turn a boat ride into a fishing trip. If you get bored out of your mind, go bottom fishing for awhile to break up the monotony. You can always mooch for Kings near the bottom and catch a few bottom fish in the process. Here are a few tips on how to insure your success with the two most popular ways to fish for Kings in the ocean.

TROLLING

Typically, trolling for kings is the more popular way to pursue a King. Depending on how many people you have on board will determine how I would suggest you plan your initial attack. If you are out there alone, which I highly recommend you are not due to safety and production reasons, your options are limited. However, if this is the case, I would always suggest trying a cut-plug troll herring. Bigger is not better in this situation fellas!:) A medium size troll Herring will be more effective due to the two hook set up will be closer placed for a strike than a big Herring and it will satisfy the King just as much. I suggest cutting the almost FROZEN Herring at an angle from behind the head at the top to a spot about a centimeter back at the bottom and also at an angle towards the bottom. Remember, the bigger the angle down, the more spin your bait will have. More spin is not always better, a floundering motion is often effective as well. Try it one way for awhile, then if that doesn't work, try it the other way. Scoop the guts out after you cut the plug. This will create more action on your bait as well. If you want to try it the "floundering" way, leave the guts in. Now that your bait is ready, AND SOAKING IN A TUB OF HERRING OR SARDINE OIL MIXTURE, rig up.

With King Salmon, you often only get one shot at a decent strike in a day. ALWAYS use a GOOD hook! Gami makes a great hook. They are expensive but worth it. There are other companies that make a good laser sharpened hook that will be ok but NEVER use a cheap hook! You just spent a pile of money to get here! 5 bucks for some good hooks to insure your success if you get a strike is CHEAP! Tie a double hook set-up with 24" to 36" of GOOD leader to a GOOD barrel swivel. I suggest Maxima or Stren for leader and a GOOD BALL BEARING SWIVEL. Do not go CHEAP on these things! You will kick yourself right square in the ass if you lose a fifty pound King salmon after trolling all day to get a bite and it breaks off because you were a CHEAP ass and bought CHEAP shit!

Place a sliding sinker up your line and tie your leader and hooks on that are tied on to your BALL BEARING swivel! Remove a troll Herring from the "brew" and put the upper hook through the gut cavity and around the backbone of the Herring and out and the "trailer" hook through the tail of the Herring in the opposite direction of the "primary" Time to fish! If you have the luxury of down riggers on your boat, simply clip your line on about 30 feet behind the boat and drop it down to about ten feet off the bottom. If you do not have any luck at that depth, adjust it every half hour or so when you check your bait. If you do not have down riggers, you will need to adjust weights accordingly to keep your bait reasonably close to the bottom. A King salmon is the bigger, slower, clumsy species of the Salmon breed. They are not as fast as their relatives like the Silver and Sockeye. You will want to troll as slow as possible yet fast enough to keep good action on your bait. If you are indeed solo out there and the

Herring isn't working after a couple hours, you have some more options. I suggest switching to a Tee-Spoon or a Skagit Special Spinner. They come in a bunch of colors and forms. I typically use either an orange body with a plain copper colored fin or an orange body with a silver and flame colored fin. Im not sure there is any real rhyme or reason to it so try whatever color suits your fancy at the time. The spinners are used just like the Herring. As slow as you can go yet still have good action on your spinner. Make sure you have a BALL BEARING swivel in the midst somewhere or you are just begging for trouble! If you have two or more anglers on the boat, I suggest using at least one set-up with a spinner in the midst. Some days the spinners are just more effective for some reason and also, I have seen more large Kings caught on Spinners than with Herring. If you are a patient fisherman and are trophy hunting, the spinner is the way to go.

MOOCHING

Mooching is another popular way to fish for King Salmon. I personally prefer this method over trolling for the simple reason that Mooching produces other fish than Kings while trying to catch your target fish. Mooching is done with the same exact set-up as for trolling with the Herring only you drop it down to the bottom with a weight on the slider, pull it up about five to ten feet off of the bottom and then jig it up and down. The benefits are both pro and con. You probably will not have as good a chance at catching a King as with trolling but you can fill your fish box with other bottom fish like Cod, Halibut, Sea Bass etc in the event you do not catch a King. Mooching is typically done in a little bit deeper water than trolling so it is ok to go on the outside of the trollers as not to interfere with their process.

With these simple ideas and tips I have laid out for you, there is no reason you cannot have a safe and successful King Salmon fishing adventure. Although I have been fishing Kings in many different waters for over 40 years, I always recommend talking to someone local to the area you are planning on fishing to get local knowledge of any dangers or advice they can give you. Thanks for reading and good luck and most importantly BE SAFE out there!

Fishing Gear (Ocean Silver)

1)   I suggest a light to medium size trolling rod that will handle 15 to 25 lb test monofilament line. I personally use a Lami-Glas, 12 to 20. You can feel the fish bite better and it's a lot more fun.

2) Silver Salmon Reel-There are a wide variety of good reels to choose from but any reputable companies levelwind that will hold a few hundred yards of 15 to 25 Lb test monofilament line will be fine.

3) Harpoon- Always carry a harpoon in case you troll into a Halibut, it just makes them easier to manage with a harpoon stuck through them. I always say, "harpoon them and you own them". (except for the time I harpooned a couple hundred pounder and then right directly shot my line and the harpoon cable in half with a .357 while attempting to kill the Halibut. No tips that day!:) Therein the .410 scattergun is a much better weapon of choice for a boat.) However, when harpooning a large Halibut in a small boat, NEVER tie the harpoon line to the boat. A large Halibut will sink your ass! Tie the end to a buoy and in the event the fish is unmanageable, toss the whole works overboard. (after making sure the line is not wrapped around your ankle of course) The fish will eventually come back to the surface with the buoy and you can easily grab it then.

4) Bait- Silver Salmon will eat pretty much anything in the ocean that will fit in their mouth when they are in abundance under the boat, you will want to bring a few options for bait for slow times. Due to certain situations that I will explain later on in this guide you will want to bring the following at a minimum.

Small Troll Herring

Herring or Sardine Oil

5) Tackle-Silver Salmon tackle for the ocean is pretty basic. If you have some double single hook rigs, medium size spinners such as Tee- Spoons, Skagit Specials etc, in a variety of colors you will be ok. For Silvers it is a good idea to have a few Pixies and Vibraxes and a good casting rod in your boat in case you run into a big school of them on the surface. Medium size sinker sliders with a variety of small sinkers and barrel and snap swivels in your box are a must as well. Do not buy cheap swivels! You are begging for a problem if you do!

6) Net- Always make sure you grab the net before you head out. Many times in my younger days I hooked into Silvers and went to grab my net and the back of my truck was too far away! It happens more often that you think!:)

Lets Go Fishing!!!

There a few important keys to the success of Silver Salmon fishing. Number one is LOCATION. Before leaving the port or beach, pull out your chart and find a good location to head for. If you are in a small boat, always look for the closest yet most productive looking area you can because if the weather gets rough you can get back to port faster. Although it is not a guy thing to do, if you are in a location you have not been before, ask somebody like a charter boat operator where the closest place to catch decent Silvers is. Typically they are going to lie to you but it's worth a shot. If you are in a brand new area, just get up early, ask around about who is the best guide service, find their boats and follow them to the grounds. It AIN'T rocket science and at 5 bucks a gallon for fuel, it will save you a bundle of money that can be spent on more important things like beer!

After deciding on a spot to head for, take a mental check list of things on board to insure your safe return and head out. Silver Salmon tend to congregate close to the beach on their way to their river of destination. There are exceptions to this rule however. "Feeder" Silvers are the ones that will stay out deeper because they are not headed for a river to spawn in. They are simply living and feeding at different locations before their trip to a spawning stream. These Silvers are best caught with downriggers and troll herring or by simply dropping a troll Herring to the bottom and mooching for them.Deeper water does not necessarily mean more Silvers so going 50 miles out definitely will not increase your luck if there are good areas closer. If you find a good area to fish reasonably close to port, head that way and give it a try. You can always move if it sucks. Finding these close spots usually is not rocket science because when you get anywhere close, there will be other boats scattered around the site. This is never a bad thing due to several reasons. The number one reason is SAFETY. The number two reason is that Silvers go where the food is and with a bunch of boats around, there is plenty of food already in the water. Its kind of a cheap shot but always go down tide of the other boats if you can find good terrain there because that is the way the other boats scent from their bait is traveling and you can cut the fish off at the pass.:) IF YOU DO ANCHOR AND MOOCH FOR SILVERS AND HALIBUT, ALWAYS BE EXTREMELY CAREFUL! THIS IS THE MOST DANGEROUS PART OF THE TRIP. MORE PEOPLE HAVE SANK IN MORE SMALL BOATS FROM IMPROPER ANCHORING AND IMPROPPER PULLING OF THE ANCHOR THAN CARTER HAS LIVER PILLS. DO NOT TRY USING THE BOUY TO PULL YOUR ANCHOR WITHOUT A TRAINED PERSON SHOWING YOU HOW TO DO IT. YOU WILL WIND UP WITH THE ANCHOR LINE IN YOUR PROP AT THE VERY LEAST AND AT THE BOTTOM OF THE OCEAN AT THE WORST!!!!

Another important aspect of Silver fishing is TIDE. Extreme high and low tides with high volumes of water moving are a pain in the ass to fish. Try to plan your trips when there is not a big difference in water volume movement from high to low tide. The biggest "wives tale" you will hear is that "SLACK" tide is the time to catch Silvers. This is WRONG! The time surrounding slack tide is however a great time to fish Kings. You want some water moving to mask your bait,hook and line and to carry scent around your location to bring in the fish. Completely slack tide is a great time to eat lunch! There is a way to liven up the action however that I will talk about in a bit.

TROLLING

Typically, trolling for Silvers is the more popular way to pursue them. Depending on how many people you have on board will determine how I would suggest you plan your initial attack. If you are out there alone, which I highly recommend you are not due to safety and production reasons, your options are limited. However, if this is the case, I would always suggest trying a cut-plug troll herring. Bigger is not better in this situation fellas!:) A small to medium size troll Herring will be more effective due to the two hook set up will be closer placed for a strike than a big Herring and it will satisfy the Silver just as much.

Page 34

I suggest cutting the almost FROZEN Herring at an angle from behind the head at the top to a spot about a centimeter back at the bottom and also at an angle towards the bottom. Remember, the bigger the angle down, the more spin your bait will have. More spin is not always better, a floundering motion is often effective as well. Try it one way for awhile, then if that doesn't work, try it the other way. Scoop the guts out after you cut the plug. This will create more action on your bait as well. If you want to try it the "floundering" way, leave the guts in. Now that your bait is ready, AND SOAKING IN A TUB OF HERRING OR SARDINE OIL MIXTURE, rig up.

ALWAYS use GOOD hooks! Gami makes a great hook. They are expensive but worth it. There are other companies that make a good laser sharpened hook that will be ok but NEVER use a cheap hook! You just spent a pile of money to get here! 5 bucks for some good hooks to insure your success if you get a strike is CHEAP! Tie a double hook set-up with 24" to 36" of GOOD leader to a GOOD barrel swivel. I suggest Maxima or Stren for leader and a GOOD BALL BEARING SWIVEL. Do not go CHEAP on these things! You will kick yourself right square in the ass if you lose a trophy Silver salmon after trolling all day to get a bite and it breaks off because you were a CHEAP ass and bought CHEAP shit!

Place a sliding sinker up your line and tie your leader and hooks on that are tied on to your BALL BEARING swivel! Remove a troll Herring from the "brew" and put the upper hook through the gut cavity and around the backbone of the Herring and out and the "trailer" hook through the tail of the Herring in the opposite direction of the "primary" Time to fish! If you have the luxury of down riggers on your boat, simply clip your line on about 30 feet behind the boat and drop it down to about ten feet off the bottom. If you do not have any luck at that depth, adjust it every half hour or so when you check your bait. If you do not have down riggers, you will need to adjust weights accordingly to keep your bait reasonably close to the bottom. A Silver salmon is the faster species of the Salmon breed. You will want to troll fast enough to keep good action on your bait. If you are indeed solo out there and the Herring isn't working after a couple hours, you have some more options. I suggest switching to a Tee-Spoon or a Skagit Special Spinner. They come in a bunch of colors and forms. I typically use either an orange body with a plain copper colored fin or an orange body with a silver and flame colored fin. Im not sure there is any real rhyme or reason to it so try whatever color suits your fancy at the time. The spinners are used just like the Herring. As slow as you can go yet still have good action on your spinner. Make sure you have a BALL BEARING swivel in the midst somewhere or you are just begging for trouble! If you have two or more anglers on the boat, I suggest using at least one set-up with a spinner in the midst. Some days the spinners are just more effective for some reason and also, I have seen more large Silvers caught on Spinners than with Herring. If you are a patient fisherman and are trophy hunting, the spinner is the way to go.

MOOCHING

Mooching is another popular way to fish for Silver Salmon. I personally prefer this method over trolling for the simple reason that Mooching produces other fish than Silvers while trying to catch your target fish. Mooching is done with the same exact set-up as for trolling with the Herring only you drop it down to the bottom with a weight on the slider, pull it up about five to ten feet off of the bottom and then jig it up and down. The benefits are both pro and con. You probably will not have as good a chance at catching a Silver as with trolling but you can fill your fish box with other bottom fish like Cod, Halibut, Sea Bass etc in the event you do not catch a Silver. Mooching is typically done in a little bit deeper water than trolling so it is ok to go on the outside of the trollers as not to interfere with their process.

CASTING

In the event that you run into a school of Silvers on the surface, grab your caster and tie on a Pixie or a Vibrax spinner. Cast into them and retrieve fairly quickly but do not "outrun" them.

PINK AND CHUM SALMON ARE THE SAME GEAR AND TECHNIQUES AS SILVER SALMON.

SOCKEYE SALMON DO NOT BITE. BRING HUGE SNAGGING HOOK AND JERK REAL HARD!!!!:)

With these simple ideas and tips I have laid out for you, there is no reason you cannot have a safe and successful Silver Salmon fishing adventure. Although I have been fishing Silvers in many different waters for over 40 years, I always recommend talking to someone local to the area you are planning on fishing to get local knowledge of any dangers or advice they can give you. Thanks for reading and good luck and most importantly BE SAFE out there!

Freshwater Sportfishing

Sportfishing Northwest Freshwater Salmon

Greetings and welcome to this edition of Northwest Sport fishing. I have over 40 years of experience fishing Northwestern waters both as a licensed guide and a private fisherman. It is not rocket science and I am just giving you a quick Crash course on how to catch fish in different areas of the Northwest.

1) King Salmon- King Salmon run from about May 15th through July 31st in the Northwest.

Rod, Reel and tackle for King Salmon in the Northwest.

Rod- Minumum line weight of 20lb test. A nice stiff graphite rod will suit you best for setting the hook and handling a nice King.

Reel- This can vary. For beginners, a large spin cast reel with a minimum of 20lb test. For more experienced anglers, a larger bait cast/levelwind with 20lb test minimum is a great way to go.

Tackle- Opinions will vary but there is one lure you will see on half the lines during King season. A flame and chartreuse Spin-n-Glow with a piece of orange yarn on the hook. Typically a size 6 for the smaller streams is most effective. Visit your local tackle store, put some size 6 Spin-n-Glows in pretied baggies on the counter and ask what has been working the best. This will do two things. The lures are very effective so you will have something to fish with that works great, AND...you wont look like a dork while you are asking the shop pro what has been working lately...:) Grab some split shot while you are there. You want your Spin-n-Glow lightly bouncing on the bottom of the river bed as it floats down. If bait is allowed, some fresh Salmon roe with your Spin-n-Glow is always a good idea but roe is not always allowed. Check the local regs. Like I said in the beginning, this ain't rocket science! If you are unsure what to do, watch the guy with the fly rod and Spin-n-Glow for five minutes before you start.......Then fish as close to him as you can without invading his space....

If you do venture into the bigger rivers in a boat for Kings, you can use the same rod and reel as above but the fishery is more of a troll fishery. You will want to take along some bigger Spin-n-Glows and some Quickfish with divers and just back troll for them. If bait is allowed, a thin strip of herring tied to your Quickfish or some salmon roe on your Spin-n-Glow is always a bonus.

Silver Salmon

Rod n Reel- A nice medium weight fly rod or spin rod and reel or baitcaster.

Silver Salmon typically run in the Northwest from mid July through the middle of September. Silver Salmon are the rudest of the Salmon species when it comes to timing. They don't own a watch apparently because the best time by far to catch them is right at dawn. Which in the Northwest in August means you gotta drag your tired ass outta bed at 3.A.M. and be on the river before sun-up around 4. Silvers have pretty much a feeding frenzy attitude right at dawn for a half hour or so. They bite predominantly on roe and the "bite" only last for about 30 to 45 minutes and then just about the time your coffee kicks in....Yep! They go to sleep! So if you haven't caught the little bastards by then, you may as well go get breakfast cuz they are DONE!:) The rest of the day can be spent flogging the water with flies or spinners or the old favorite (Spin-n-Glow but its a tough row to hoe! The good news is, typically when the Silvers are running, so are the Pinks. And Pinks are the dumbest fish in the food chain but will break up the monotony........

Pink Salmon

Rod n Reel- Same as Silvers.....

Im not sure how many of you are familiar with a spruce chicken, (grouse), but the Pink Salmon is along those lines of the fish food chain. They are dumber than a box of rocks! However, when the Silvers aren't biting, the Pinks will fill in the blank time of flogging the water. They are a bit smaller than the Silver Salmon and not the fighter, but they can be entertaining and it doesnt take much angling to get one to bite. They are great for kids! The Pinks start running in all the Northwest streams around July first and are pretty well wiped out by the end of August. Pinks are not much of a food fish, (kinda mushy) but are a great in between, game fish. Spinners, flies, spoons etc. are all effective.

Sockeye Salmon

For Sockeye (Red) Salmon fishing you can use the same rod and reel as above. Red fishing is a bit different in the aspect of this species does not like to bite so you have to snag them in the mouth. This is best done with a floating bead just above your hook and a few sinkers about 18 inches above that. The theory is that the weights keep the main line on the bottom but the bead floats downstream a little off of the bottom and will float the line into the sockeyes mouth. Some areas restrict bead use so you can use any fly made out of hollow hair. The hollow hair will float your fly up off the bottom just like a bead.

Trout

Fly or Trout Rod

The Northwest has several Trout species. Salmon roe where it is allowed is always a favorite bait. Spinners, spoons and flies are also effective on the species. They are a fun fish to catch on light tackle and another big favorite for the kids.

Keep in mind there are many lakes and streams in the Northwest that are great Trout fishing and places just to relax and enjoy what the Northwest has to offer.......

That about wraps it up for the Crash course on where and how for the do it yourself fisherpeopleIf you have any questions that I haven't answered, feel free to shoot me an email at crash.davis99@yahoo.com and I will try to answer it and make sure I earn your 5 bucks☐. I have over 40 years of fishing these local water and can answer pretty much any question you may have. Thanks and Good Luck and tight lines....Crash....

If you have any questions, feel free to email me at crash.davis99@yahoo.com......

OH! I almost forgot! Here is a picture/diagram for the asswipe that left me shitty feed back for not having any   pictures……

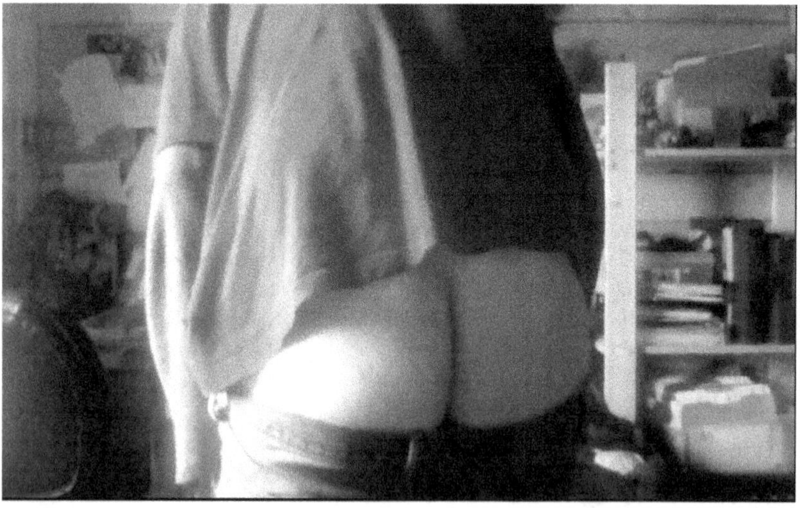

ANY QUESTIONS??? Good Luck out there…..CRASH…..